THE NANO-CHANGE PROWESS

Transforming The Ordinary For Maximum Impact

Jimmy L. McIntosh

INTRODUCTION

Unveiling The Power Of NanoChange

The euphoric stream of unfathomable joy in my heart to pen down this precious information to you is beyond telling. The information expressed in this book is carefully written based on an experience I had and the true story of a dear beloved sister. Her story pushed me to do further studies and research about NanoChange and its corresponding power as a businessman. Her exuberance is just amazing in pushing further in so many things, especially as an artist.

In a bustling city where change was the only constant, my friend and sister with that humble spirit named Lily found herself at a crossroads in her life. Lily is an amazing Artist who yearned for a way to enhance her artistry, to breathe life into her creativity, and to carve a niche in the competitive world of art. Feeling overwhelmed by the enormity of her aspirations, she sought guidance from an unexpected source – My mentor whom I hadn't heard from in the past four years. Professor Mcdonald. It surprised my heart to know that Lily had a connection with Professor Mcdonald. Professor McDonald has one of the old bookstores in the town.

As Lily wandered through the narrow aisles of the bookstore, her eyes were drawn to a book with a vibrant cover that seemed to pulse with energy. The title read "NanoMoves: Unleashing the Artistic Spirit Within." Intrigued, she picked it up and began to read. At this point, when Lily was describing how she came across that book it was as though a force was dragging her to that area. I know Professor Mcdonald as a visionary man. Therefore, his books must contain some energy to make people mighty.

The pages of this amazing book unfolded a captivating narrative of a painter named Alex who, like Lily, sought to elevate his expertise in art. Alex was introduced to the concept of "NanoMoves" by his mentor, a seasoned artist known for pushing boundaries in the art world. "NanoMoves," the mentor explained, were small, deliberate actions or adjustments that could profoundly impact the craft. With each carefully planned brushstroke, Alex applied his newfound understanding of "NanoMoves" to his art. He meticulously adjusted the intensity of colors, the texture of strokes, and the composition of his pieces. Small changes, but each one transformed his paintings from ordinary to extraordinary. He realized that by mastering these tiny, deliberate alterations, he was achieving "Expertise Elevation" in his artistic journey.

The story resonated with Lily deeply. It was an epiphany—a revelation that in her quest for artistic growth, she need not feel overwhelmed by grand, sweeping changes. Instead, she could embrace the power of "NanoMoves" – those minuscule yet impactful alterations that could revolutionize her approach to art. I know my sister, Lily.

Lily began to apply this newfound wisdom to her own. She experimented with subtle shifts in color palettes, refined the details of her sketches, and reconsidered her perspective on various art techniques. As she progressed, she marveled at the significant difference these "NanoMoves" made in her creations. Each piece became a testament to her journey of "Expertise Elevation," showcasing the immense potential of small, purposeful changes. AndAse city's art scene bore witness to Lily's remarkable transformation, her story inspired aspiring artists to embrace the magic of "NanoMoves" and embark on their ney towards mastery.

In the following pages, we delve deeper into the art of "NanoMoves" and "Expertise Elevation' as my sister, Lily discovered and it worked for her. As a businessman, I'm diving deeper with you on this journey through strategies, and practical applications, I unlock the immense potential these concepts hold. Join me on this enlightening journey, where we celebrate the notion that even the tiniest brushstrokes can paint the grandest masterpieces. Your life and business will experience a great transformation and launch you into your highest potential for maximum impact.

CHAPTER 1

COMPONENTS OF CONDUCT

As a businessman who seeks to produce the quality of things to men across the globe, it's of a necessity to understand the components of conduct concerning each person I come in contact with. Your ability to understand the way someone acts and behaves is your strength to partnership with such a person. It's in the components of conduct that we are able to build up that intelligence of knowing the character that governs people, understanding how they act and react, especially when there is a situation. Knowing these things about the person makes you come into the light of awareness and responsibility. What are the components of conduct? Fundamentally, components of conduct allude to the key parts that impact how people act, think, and respond in different circumstances. These components envelop mental, humanistic, and physiological angles, molding humans directly. In this chapter, I don't want to bore you with a lot of words but go straight to the point. These are seven (7) components of conduct which personally I have picked upon myself to study.

1. COGNITION

Cognition encapsulates mental processes such as thinking, perception, memory, reasoning, and problem-solving. It's how individuals interpret and navigate the world. Perception allows them to process sensory information, shaping their understanding of reality. Memory enables them to retain and recall experiences, informing decision-making. Thinking and reasoning guide problem-solving and judgments, influencing behavior based on cognitive evaluation. This is very essential in the life of a person, especially a businessman or businesswoman. The power of cognition, the mental processes that underpin our understanding of the world, is profound and transformative. It influences how we interpret information, make decisions, and navigate our lives as stated already. A compelling real-life experience illustrating this power is the story of Helen Keller, a remarkable woman who overcame the challenges of deaf-blindness to become a prominent author, lecturer, and advocate. This is one of the stories I have read that pushed me into unbreakable determination in my quest as a businessman and mentor in the space of relationships.

Helen Keller, born in 1880, lost her vision and hearing at the age of 19 months due to an illness. She was trapped in a world of silence and darkness, unable to communicate or comprehend the world as others did. However, with the assistance of her teacher, Anne Sullivan, Helen began to unlock the power of cognition. This sounds interesting, right?

Anne Sullivan introduced Helen to a new way of understanding the world by using touch to teach her language. Through finger-spelling words into Helen's palm, Anne conveyed meanings and concepts, enabling Helen to grasp the idea that each word represented an object, action, or emotion. This breakthrough ignited Helen's cognitive processes, allowing her to understand and communicate.

As Helen's cognition developed, her world expanded exponentially. She learned to read Braille, to write, and eventually to speak. Through books and education, her mind blossomed, and she became an advocate for education and opportunities for the disabled. Helen Keller's life exemplifies the power of cognition to transcend physical limitations, demonstrating that the mind's capacity to learn and adapt is immense.

This story underscores how cognition enables us to perceive, learn, and adapt to our circumstances. It shows that with the right stimulus and guidance, individuals can overcome immense challenges and achieve greatness. Cognition empowers us to learn from experiences, communicate with others, and shape our lives. It's a testament to the incredible potential and resilience of the human mind, capable of turning adversity into strength and transforming lives in profound ways. This is a master key to unlock uninterrupted talents, ideas, and potential for a maximum impact.

2. EMOTIONS

Emotions are very powerful. When you rightfully use your emotions the results are inevitable. What you feel creates your course of interactions. Knowing how to govern your emotions well in the place of intelligence makes you an icon in your world. The reason is because your energy is in motion. The movement of your energy. Where you channel the energy to is the most cardinal matter. Wherever energy is released and focused to produce a particular result based on what is concentrated in the person's mind and heart. Whatever you feel has within it an informative bank. What do I mean? What I mean is that your emotions are signals of information at a specific time. Knowing how to govern your emotions helps you to make a maximum impact. One of the greatest ways of handling people and impacting their lives is to understand their emotions. What they feel has something to say about their current state. Emotions are complex psychological states triggered by various stimuli, experiences, or thoughts. These states, such as joy, fear, anger, sadness, and love, significantly impact behavior and decision-making. Emotions often arise unconsciously but profoundly influence actions, interactions, and relationships. The rising of emotions unconsciously can be intelligently handled and governed through a conscious mind. Imagine someone gets you angry and you consciously decide not to be angry and react. These are emotions! You want to be financially stable. That's not a bad idea. But how do you feel about money? You want to achieve about $ 2,000 in your business life, yet your feeling about $ 2,000 does not reflect that amount of money because when you hear $ 2,000, in your heart fear has risen. Your emotions are as cardinal and important as your success, impact, and your maintainability of your success.

To control and govern your emotions intelligently adopt these strategies:

- Self-awareness

- Acceptance without judgment

- Pause and Reflect

- Practice deep breathing and relaxation

- Exercise and Healthy lifestyle

- Express Emotions Constructively

- Developing Coping Strategies

- Mindfulness and Meditation

- Seek Professional Help

- Set Boundaries

- Positive affirmation and gratitude

- Empathy and understanding others

3. MOTIVATION

I personally see motivation as a kind of virtue which gives vitality to someone to perform an action or accomplish a work. Motivation is the driving force that propels individuals towards action, accomplishment, and the pursuit of goals. It is the spark that energizes and sustains effort, enabling people to overcome obstacles and achieve success. Understanding the mechanisms and facets of motivation is essential for personal growth, professional success, and a fulfilling life. It is fueled by internal factors like needs, desires, and interests, as well as external incentives such as rewards or recognition. Motivation varies in intensity and is influenced by personal and environmental dynamics. Know WHAT motivates you internally and WHO motivates you externally.

4. SOCIAL INFLUENCE

Social influence examines how interactions with others, societal norms, and cultural context shape behavior and decision-making. People often align their actions with group norms or expectations, seeking social approval or avoiding disapproval. Understanding social influence is crucial in comprehending behaviors in diverse social settings. Let's look at the types of social influence, Factors Contributing to social influence, Channels of social influence, The positive and negative Aspects of social influence.

● **Types of Social Influence**

Normative Influence:
This occurs when individuals conform to the expectations or norms of a group to gain acceptance, approval, or avoid social rejection.

Informational Influence:
This happens when individuals rely on others' actions or opinions to obtain information and make decisions, especially in ambiguous or uncertain situations.

Identification Influence: Individuals align their behaviors and beliefs with a specific group or individual they admire, respect, or wish to be associated with.

Internalization Influence: This involves a deep integration of others' beliefs or attitudes into one's own value system, leading to genuine adoption of those beliefs.

• Factors contributing to Social Influence

Group Dynamics: The size, cohesion, and structure of a group influence the extent of its impact on an individual.

Expertise and Credibility: Individuals are more likely to be influenced by those perceived as experts or credible sources of information.

Social Norms: Established behavioral norms within a society or group heavily influence individual behavior and decisions.

Culture and Background: Cultural beliefs, traditions, and societal backgrounds shape the ways people are influenced and the norms they adhere to.

● Channels of Social Influence

Direct Social Interaction: Face-to-face conversations, discussions, and debates with others can significantly impact one's beliefs and behaviors.

Media and Technology: Mass media, social media, and online platforms play a significant role in shaping public opinion and influencing behavior.

Peer Pressure: The influence exerted by peers can be powerful, especially during adolescence, affecting choices related to fashion, lifestyle, and behavior.

● Positive and Negative aspects of Social Influence

Positive Influence: It can inspire positive behaviors like charitable acts, altruism, and social activism, leading to societal development and cohesion.

Negative Influence: Social influence can also lead to detrimental behaviors, such as conformity to harmful norms or participation in unethical activities due to peer pressure.

I believe these will encourage a balanced approach, enabling you to discern and align with positive influences while resisting negative ones.

5. PERSONALITY

Personality refers to a distinctive and enduring set of individual traits, patterns of behavior, thoughts, emotions, and characteristics that define a person's unique identity and how they interact with the world. It encompasses a wide array of psychological aspects that shape how individuals perceive, interpret, and respond to various situations, making it a fundamental aspect of human experience. You can not make a maximum impact beyond what you have become. Let's dive into the components of personality, theories of personality, development and change in personality, Understanding Personality for Growth and Relationship, and Cultural and Individual Variation.

● Components Of Personality

Traits: These are enduring qualities that remain relatively stable over time, such as extroversion, agreeableness, conscientiousness, neuroticism, and openness to experience.

Behavioral Patterns: Consistent ways in which individuals act across different situations, reflecting their habitual responses and actions.

Cognition: How an individual processes information, thinks, reasons, and perceives the world.

Emotions: The range, intensity, and expression of emotional responses to different stimuli and events.

Motives and Values: The driving forces that guide behavior and decision-making, reflecting an individual's priorities and goals.

● Theories Of Personality

Trait Theories: These posit that personality can be understood through identifying and measuring consistent traits that define an individual's behavior.

Psychoanalytic Theories: Sigmund Freud's psychoanalytic theory emphasizes the role of the unconscious mind, asserting that unconscious thoughts and desires influence behavior.

Humanistic Theories: These focus on personal growth, self-actualization, and the inherent goodness of individuals, as seen in Abraham Maslow's hierarchy of needs and Carl Rogers' person-centered approach.

Social-Cognitive Theories: These theories highlight the interaction between personal factors (traits), behavior, and environmental influences, such as Albert Bandura's social-cognitive theory.

• Development and Change in Personality

Personality evolves over a lifetime, influenced by experiences, relationships, education, and environmental factors. Significant life events, trauma, or major transitions can impact personality, prompting shifts in behavior and perspective.

● **Understanding Personality for Growth and Relationships**

Understanding one's own personality helps in personal growth, self-awareness, and making informed decisions aligned with one's values and aspirations.
Understanding others' personalities improves interpersonal relationships, communication, and collaboration by appreciating diverse perspectives and adapting communication styles accordingly.

● **Cultural and Individual Variation**

Culture significantly influences personality, shaping norms, values, and behaviors that are characteristic of a particular society or group.

Despite cultural influence, each individual's personality is unique and shaped by a combination of genetic, environmental, and personal factors.

Appreciating the complexity and richness of personality allows individuals to embrace their uniqueness, understand others more empathetically, and navigate the intricacies of human interactions and relationships effectively. It is a multifaceted aspect of humanity that contributes to the diversity and beauty of the human experience.

6. LEARNING

Learning is a multifaceted process that involves acquiring knowledge, skills, behaviors, attitudes, or understanding through various means and experiences. It's a fundamental aspect of human development and adaptation, shaping our responses to the world and influencing how we navigate and interact with our environment. Progressively, you become what you're learning. Whatever you learn exposes your capacity, intelligence, character, and your ways of conduct. Your behavior in learning and what you're learning determines your course of success. Learning is one of the vital essences of your becoming, as a businessman, leader, mother, father, teacher, etc. One essential truth I always tell my mentees is that, you can not impact what you don't have and what you have not become. Whatever you have learned in the course of your life serves as the stepping stone to be impactful and express your enriching potential. Whatever you have learnt can be read in every expression you make, whether by way of doing business, relationship, marriage, trading, communication, etc. Your learning capacity and ability serve as pillars of your progress in the courses of life. There are various aspects of learning,

• Acquisition of Knowledge and Skills

• Adaptation and Behavior Modification

• Experience and Exposure

• Memory and Retention

• Formal and Informal Learning

- Continuous And Lifelong Process

- Cognitive and Behavioral Learning Theories

- Application and Transfer of Learning

- Motivation and Learning, etc.

Learning is a universal asset in every kind of field. Submerge yourself into accurate learning of the right information for a tremendous transformation and make a maximum impact in everything around you.

7. GENETICS AND BIOLOGY

Genetics and biology involve inherent biological factors and genetic predispositions that influence behavior. These factors include instincts, genetic traits, and neurological processes. Genetic predispositions can affect personality traits, cognitive abilities, and susceptibility to certain conditions, all of which play a role in shaping behavior and responses. Biological influences provide insights into the intricate relationship between biology and behavior. Understanding these elements contributes to a holistic understanding of human behavior and how it is influenced by both intrinsic and extrinsic factors.

In the rudimentary information provided to you in this chapter, I strongly believe your ways of perception are transformed into paramount visions. I will surely see you at the top of life.

CHAPTER 2

THE SCIENCE OF SMALL CHANGES

Science is a broad concept and field of study. However, in the context of 'small changes' science refers to a systematic and evidence-based approach to understanding, implementing, and optimizing minor adjustments or alterations that can have a significant impact. It involves the application of scientific principles, research findings, and data analysis to explore the potential outcomes and effectiveness of making small modifications in various aspects of life. In the vast landscape of personal development and self-improvement, the power of small changes often goes underestimated. We are drawn to the allure of monumental transformations, overlooking the fact that significant shifts can stem from the smallest of actions. In this chapter, we delve into the science behind these seemingly minor alterations and how they can orchestrate profound impacts on our lives. I remember when I first started writing and moving as a strategic speaker, I was turned down several times and faced hectic rejections. Based on these experiences I discovered an atomic or small change which launched me into a buoyant recognition of my potential and knowledge as an author, strategic speaker, and businessman.

THE BUTTERFLY EFFECT AND CHAOTIC SYSTEMS

In chaos theory, a branch of mathematics and physics, there's a principle known as the "Butterfly Effect." It suggests that small changes in initial conditions can lead to vastly different outcomes in a nonlinear system. The metaphorical idea is that the flap of a butterfly's wings in Brazil could set off a chain of events leading to a tornado in Texas. This notion underscores the interconnectedness of all things and the ripple effect of even the slightest actions.

Similarly, in our lives, seemingly inconsequential decisions and actions can set off a chain reaction, influencing our trajectory in unexpected ways. A small change in habits, routines, or mindset can trigger a series of events that lead to substantial transformations over time. Understanding this concept empowers us to appreciate the potency of minor adjustments in our daily lives. The Butterfly effect is such a powerful principle that can set on a large scale of unfathomable success.

NEURAL PLASTICITY: REWIRING THE BRAIN

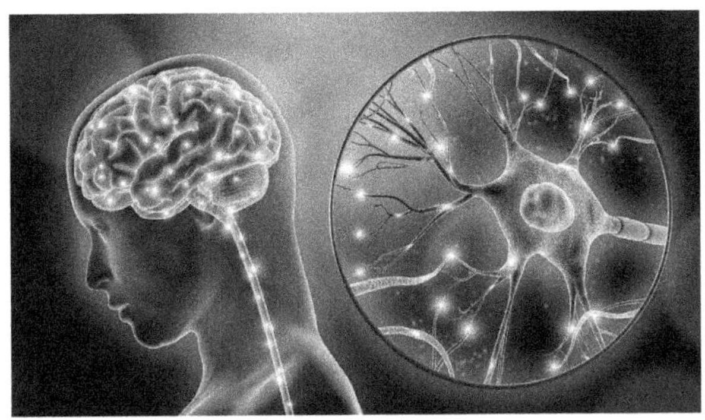

Our brains possess a remarkable ability known as neural plasticity or brain plasticity. It refers to the brain's capacity to reorganize its structure, function, and connections in response to experiences, learning, and environmental changes. When we make small changes, whether in behavior, thought patterns, or learning, we are essentially rewiring our brains. Each time we engage in a new activity or adjust our routine, neural pathways are formed or strengthened in the brain. Over time, these pathways become more efficient, making the adapted behavior more natural and automatic. Hence, by consciously introducing small positive changes, we are gradually sculpting our brain to align with our desired habits and goals. This produces prestigious results and to make a maximum impact.

HABIT FORMATION AND THE POWER OF CONSISTENCY

Whatever you consistently do builds your habit. Consistency is the building blocks of your habit. What feeds into your habit through consistency is energy. Scientifically, energy is the ability to do work. Consistency is one of the greatest works you have to own. This is because by consistency you can own any form of business enterprise. Consistency must serve as a foundation that is solidified. Habits, deeply ingrained behaviors, are fundamental aspects of our daily lives. They shape our routines, influence our choices, and ultimately define our character. The process of habit formation relies on a psychological loop involving a cue, routine, and reward. Small changes often target this loop to help create or modify habits effectively.

When we introduce small, manageable adjustments to our routines and behaviors, we establish a foundation for forming new, positive habits. By consistently reinforcing these changes, we strengthen the habit loop, making it easier to sustain the desired behavior over time. As these adjustments become habitual, their impact compounds, leading to substantial improvements in the long run. You can not use any form of habit to eradicate consistency. Consistency is the force that makes your habit effective. Introducing small changes with the power of consistency can make room for infilling of new potentials and great achievements in every sector of your life.

BEHAVIORAL ECONOMICS AND NUDGING

Behavioral economics explores how psychological, social, and cognitive factors influence the economic decisions and behaviors of individuals and institutions. Within this realm lies the concept of "nudging," a subtle yet powerful technique. A nudge is a gentle push or suggestion that influences decision-making without imposing restrictions or mandates.

Small changes in the way choices are presented or framed can significantly impact decisions. By understanding human behavior and employing carefully crafted nudges, individuals can steer themselves and others toward better choices and outcomes. These nudges, often unobtrusive, can guide us towards positive changes in health, finances, and various other aspects of life.

In conclusion of this chapter, The science of small changes reveals that impactful transformations don't always require monumental efforts. By understanding the dynamics of chaos theory, neural plasticity, habit formation, and behavioral economics, which i have applied in my personal life and it worked amazingly for me. we can harness the potential of small, deliberate alterations in our lives. Each minor adjustment sets in motion a cascade of effects, allowing us to mold our habits, routines, and perspectives into pathways that lead to personal growth and success.

CHAPTER 3

UNEARTHING AND DISCOVERING YOUR NANO-CHANGE POTENTIALS

In the heart of every individual lies a potential for growth and transformation, waiting to be harnessed. Just as a seed holds the promise of a magnificent tree, each person carries within them the possibility of remarkable change. This chapter explores the concept of "NanoChange" and how to unlock the immense potential within, discovering the power of tiny, purposeful adjustments in our lives.

UNDERSTANDING THE ESSENCE OF NANO-CHANGE

Imagine a sculptor strictly chiseling down at a block of marble. Each precise strike of the chisel represents a thoughtful and deliberate adaptation, gradually revealing the masterpiece hidden within the gravestone. Also, in the realm of particular growth and moxie elevation," NanoChange" are those finely calculated adaptations that bring out the stylish in us. A" NanoChange" is a conscious and deliberate small step or revision, frequently putatively insignificant on its own, but when integrated into our lives, it can yield profound results. These Micro-adjustments can be applied to colorful aspects of our lives, whether it's our habits, mindset, chops, or connections. They're the structure blocks of progress, the incremental shifts that, over time, accumulate into significant advancements. NanoChanges are keys.

EMBRACING THE POTENTIAL OF NANO-CHANGE

Discovering our potential for "NanoChanges" requires a willingness to explore and a readiness to embrace change. It begins with acknowledging that even the smallest actions and alterations can exert a meaningful influence on our lives. This awareness paves the way for recognizing the countless opportunities for "NanoChanges" in our daily routines and endeavors.

Start by reflecting on your goals, aspirations, and the areas of your life you wish to enhance. Whether it's improving your health, honing a skill, enriching relationships, or advancing your career, identify the small changes that, when consistently applied, could propel you towards your objectives. These could be actions as simple as dedicating a few minutes each day to practice, adopting a healthier dietary choice, or scheduling regular check-ins with loved ones. This is something I personally embarked on, and it greatly helped me in my business and mentoring career.

UNLEASHING YOUR NANO-CHANGE POTENTIAL

A potential that lies dormant in a person is not entirely wasteful but ineffective in the sense that it's not discovered to be used in order to make an impact and produce results.

To unleash your "NanoChange" potential, follow these fundamental steps:

1. *Self-Reflection*

Begin by introspecting and identifying the areas of your life you want to improve. Consider your values, aspirations, and the aspects that align with your long-term vision.

2. *Goal Setting*

Set specific, achievable goals that align with your reflections. Break down your objectives into smaller, manageable milestones.

3. *Identify NanoChanges*

Analyze the goals you've set and identify the small, meaningful adjustments you can make to move closer to them. These could be daily actions, mindset shifts, or changes in your routine.

4. *Create an Action Plan*

Develop a structured action plan incorporating these "NanoChange." Outline the steps you will take, the frequency of these actions, and how you'll track your progress.

5. *Implement Consistently*

Commit to integrating these "NanoMoves" into your daily routine. Consistency is key to making them a habit and experiencing their transformative impact.

6. **Monitor and Adjust**

Regularly evaluate your progress. Celebrate the successes and learn from any setbacks. Adjust your approach as needed, fine-tuning your "NanoMoves" for optimal results.

THE YOUNG PROFESSIONAL SPEAKER: SARAH'S NANO-CHANGE JOURNEY

Sarah Loverson is a very amazing friend of mine whose understanding concerning various strategies of business and life is outstanding. Yet, Sarah needed something more than what she knew and understood. I showed Sarah the principles of NanoChanges. Sarah, a young professional aspiring to improve her public speaking skills, embarked on her "NanoChange" journey. Her main goal was to conquer her fear of public speaking and enhance her confidence in presenting ideas. It's quite surprising that Sarah is a good, intelligent and skillful speaker and yet has fears in public speaking. Sarah's NanoChanges was a simple yet powerful action as I taught her: every day, she would practice speaking in front of a mirror for just five minutes as she imagined a large audience in a big hall. Over time, this small daily practice helped her feel more at ease, improve her articulation, refine her delivery, and accelerate her impact in a great proportion.

NanoChange encapsulates the spirit of growth, illustrating that even the tiniest actions, when purposefully executed and consistently applied, can yield significant and transformative outcomes. Discovering your "NanoChange" potential involves embracing the idea that change is not only attainable but also can be accomplished through the power of small, deliberate adjustments. In the journey towards mastery and expertise elevation, let the concept of "NanoChangs" guide you, enabling you to unlock your potential and reach new heights in all aspects of your life just as Sarah applied these principles. You're on a journey of great success and impact.

CHAPTER 4

CRAFTING YOUR NANO-CHANGE BLUEPRINT

In this chapter I want to begin with a story of one of the mentees who continually put a smile on my face. In the heart of a buzzing city, amidst towering skyscrapers and bustling streets, lived Mark, a young entrepreneur with big dreams and an insatiable appetite for success. Mark had always envisioned creating a revolutionary product that would change lives and disrupt the market. He had the vision, the drive, and the team, but he felt lost in the vastness of his ambitions.

One fateful afternoon, as he pondered over a cup of coffee, he stumbled upon an article that spoke of a concept called "NanoChange." That was my first article written. The idea was simple yet profound – making small, deliberate changes, or "NanoMoves," to bring about significant improvements. Inspired by this revelation, Mark decided to apply the concept to his business aspirations and craft his very own

"NanoChange Blueprint." When Mark applied this concept of "NanoChange", he further sought my mentor. It's been an amazing turnaround for Mark as he keeps making great impact and outstanding success.

THE BIRTH OF NANO-CHANGE

Through my mentorship class with Mark, Mark believed that the true essence of change lay in its subtlety. Just as a gentle breeze can set a thousand leaves in motion, so too could a well-planned NanoChange set a business on a transformative trajectory.

The first step was to identify the areas within his business that could benefit from these nano-level modifications. He analyzed every aspect - from product design and customer service to marketing strategies and team dynamics. He soon realized that by focusing on the smallest units of change within each domain, he could instigate a ripple effect of transformation. I will talk more about the ripple effect in chapter Six(6).

THE ANATOMY OF NANO-CHANGE

Creating a NanoChange was akin to sculpting a masterpiece from a block of marble. It required precision, insight, and a clear vision of the end result. During one of our classes, I taught Mark the four crucial elements that defined the anatomy of a NanoChange.

1. Clarity of Purpose

Every NanoChange needed a clear objective. In the course of studies, I helped Mark to identify what he aimed to achieve with each NanoMove - whether it was enhancing user experience, optimizing processes, or boosting team morale. Clarity of purpose provided the compass to guide these nano-level alterations.

2. Deliberate Selection

A NanoChange wasn't about changing everything at once. It involved carefully selecting a specific element, no matter how small, that could make a substantial difference. It was about focusing on a single brushstroke that would enhance the entire painting.

3. **Strategic Placement**

Just as the placement of each stroke on a canvas mattered, so did the strategic placement of NanoMoves or NanoChange. I made Mark understand that where these small changes were implemented mattered as much as what was changed. It required foresight and analysis to position these NanoMoves for maximum impact.

4. **Measurable Impact**

Every NanoChange needed to be measurable. Mark realized the importance of setting clear metrics to assess the impact of each NanoMove during the course. Whether it was an increase in user engagement, a reduction in response time, or a boost in productivity, these measurable outcomes provided invaluable insights into the effectiveness of the NanoChange. Now let's into the crafting process

THE CRAFTING PROCESS

Armed with this newfound understanding as I journey with Mark through the world of NanoChange, Mark began crafting his NanoChange Blueprint. He gathered his team and initiated brainstorming sessions, encouraging each member to contribute their thoughts and insights. They collectively identified areas that needed refinement and started brainstorming NanoMoves to address these issues. These are the steps I unfolded to Mark in one of our sessions.

Step 1: Identifying Opportunities

The first task was to identify opportunities for NanoChange. I told Mark to encourage his team to assess their current processes and practices critically. Were there bottlenecks in their workflow? Could user experience be enhanced? Were there pain points in their product that needed attention? These questions sparked ideas for potential NanoMoves.

Step 2: Ideation and Selection

With a list of opportunities, the team dove into an ideation phase. They brainstormed and generated a plethora of NanoMove ideas, ranging from streamlining their customer support response time to tweaking the user interface for a more intuitive experience. The key was to have a multitude of options to choose from.

Once they had a range of ideas, they evaluated each based on feasibility, potential impact, and alignment with their overall business objectives. They carefully selected a handful of NanoMoves that stood out as high-impact and achievable. It was an amazing watch view of Mark and his team progress.

Step 3: Blueprint Creation

With the selected NanoMoves in hand, they proceeded to create their NanoChange Blueprint. The blueprint included a detailed plan for each NanoMove, outlining the specific actions, the desired outcomes, the metrics to measure success, and the timeline for implementation.

THE POWER OF NANO-CHANGE UNLEASHED

With their NanoChange Blueprint in place, Mark and his team began implementing the selected NanoMoves. It was incredible to witness the power of these seemingly minuscule alterations. The once overwhelming goal of transforming their business had become a series of manageable, focused actions. They tracked the progress meticulously and celebrated even the smallest victories. Each NanoMove and NanoChange that was successfully implemented nudged them closer to their ultimate vision as I taught Mark. The efficiency of their customer support improved, user engagement skyrocketed, and internal communication became more streamlined. That sounds amazing, right?

A REVOLUTION IN THE MAKING

Finally, Through this journey of crafting their NanoChange Blueprint, Mark realized that real change didn't always demand drastic, Herculean efforts. By focusing on the tiniest elements and making deliberate, strategic alterations, he was shaping a revolution within his business. The ripple effect of these NanoMoves and NanoChanges resonated throughout his organization, bringing about a transformation that was both inspiring and empowering.

Embrace the concept of NanoChange, and let it be the catalyst for your journey towards mastery, one deliberate NanoMove at a time. Your success is assured.

CHAPTER 5

OVERCOMING RESISTANCE AND BUILDING RESILIENCE

In the grand tapestry of personal growth and transformation, resistance often emerges as a formidable adversary. It's the force that opposes change, making us question our capabilities and discouraging us from pursuing our goals. However, within the context of "NanoMoves or NanoChanges" and "Expertise Elevation," resistance can be reframed as a stepping stone toward growth, and resilience as the sturdy bridge that guides us over it. I remember that particular night, where I was bombarded with a lot of thoughts, feeling rejected, confused, and frustrated because nothing seemed to work. However, it was through this darkest night of my life I discovered NanoChange and NanoMoves. How did I do that in the first place? I recognised the resistance.

- **Recognizing Resistance**

Resistance manifests in various forms. It can be the doubt that creeps into our minds when faced with a new challenge or the procrastination that veils our determination. It's the fear of failure that paralyzes us and the voice within that whispers, "You're not good enough." This resistance can be crippling, halting progress and stifling potential. However, understanding that resistance is a natural reaction to change is the first step towards conquering it. It's an indicator that we're venturing beyond our comfort zones, challenging ourselves, and on the cusp of growth. In the realm of "NanoMoves and NanoChanges" resistance should be viewed as an invitation to persevere, to apply small adjustments and continue forging ahead.

- **Embracing the Power of NanoMoves in Overcoming Resistance**

"NanoMoves and NanoChanges" provide a unique strategy for overcoming resistance. When faced with a daunting task or a persistent resistance, instead of succumbing to the pressure, break it down into minuscule parts. Identify the smallest, manageable actions you can take. By dissecting the challenge into tiny components, the resistance loses its overwhelming power, and each mini-action becomes achievable. For instance, if you're resisting starting a new project, begin with the tiniest of steps—perhaps writing a single sentence or brainstorming a single idea. These minor actions accumulate, gradually eroding resistance and propelling you forward. Overcoming resistance through "NanoMoves and NanoChanges" is about taking consistent, small steps, persistently and purposefully.

THE ROLE OF RESILIENCE EXPERTISE ELEVATION

Resilience is the backbone of expertise elevation. It's the ability to bounce back from setbacks, adapt to change, and maintain determination amidst challenges. Building resilience is crucial in the pursuit of mastery, as it safeguards against the detrimental effects of resistance. To foster resilience, it's essential to cultivate a growth mindset. View challenges as opportunities for learning and growth rather than insurmountable obstacles. Embrace failures as stepping stones towards success and use them to refine your approach with the right perceptions.

STRATEGIES FOR ENHANCING RESILIENCE

1. Mindfulness and Self-awareness

Understand your reactions to resistance. Cultivate mindfulness to recognize when resistance arises and observe how it manifests. Self-awareness enables you to respond, rather than react, effectively. Your response to a particular resistance determines your ability to handle the resistance.

2. Positive Affirmations and Visualization

Incorporate positive affirmations and visualization techniques into your daily routine. Affirm your capabilities and envision successful outcomes. This cultivates a positive mindset, enhancing resilience.

3. Physical Health and Well-being

Prioritize physical health through regular exercise, a balanced diet, and sufficient rest. A healthy body supports a healthy mind, contributing to greater resilience.

4. Community and Support

Surround yourself with a supportive community of like-minded individuals. Sharing experiences, insights, and encouragement creates a network of strength that bolsters resilience.

THE SYNERGY OF NANO-CHANGES AND RESILIENCE

When "NanoChange" and resilience converge, an unstoppable force is created. "NanoChange" breaks down resistance into manageable fragments, and resilience empowers us to navigate through them with fortitude. It's a symbiotic relationship that fuels progress, propelling us towards our aspirations.

In the grand journey of expertise elevation, resistance and resilience are not adversaries but companions. Resistance highlights the areas for growth, and resilience equips us to face those challenges head-on, fortified by the power of "NanoChange"

As you embrace the journey of "Expertise Elevation" armed with "NanoMoves" and a resilient spirit, you'll find that the road to mastery is not just about reaching the destination but about developing into your best self en route. Together, let's unlock the profound impact that small, purposeful actions can have in overcoming resistance and building resilience on the path to mastery as I have applied these principles to my life and others.

CHAPTER 6

THE RIPPLES EFFECT: HOW NANO-CHANGE CREATES LARGE WAVES

In the heart of a bustling metropolis, Vanessa, a young social activist, stood on a crowded street corner, advocating for environmental sustainability. Armed with passion and determination, she sought to create a positive change in her community. Vanessa believed in the power of collective action and the significance of every small step towards a greener future.

Vanessa's story is a testament to the transformative effect of what we call "NanoChange." At first glance, these actions may seem insignificant, but when multiplied and adopted by many, they create a ripple effect—a force for lasting, significant change. This book is all about practicality. That's why I bring true stories to the scene in order to align these information with your life.

THE POWER OF THE TINY DROPS

There is a famous quote which has gone across most civilizations. Julia Carney quoted, "Little drops of water make a mighty ocean." Imagine a still pond. When a tiny drop breaks its surface, it creates a ripple—a ripple that starts small but grows larger, reaching the farthest corners of the pond. Similarly, in the realm of personal and societal change, every small action—every nano-change—sends out ripples that affect the world around us.

Small Actions, Big Impact

NanoMoves are like the initial droplets in that pond, causing a series of reactions that amplify over time. When Sarah decided to start a community garden in her neighborhood, she planted a seed—literally and metaphorically. This act was a nano-change, a seemingly minor step. Yet, it set off a chain of events that rippled through her community.

People became inspired by her garden and began planting their own. Soon, a once desolate neighborhood bloomed into an oasis of greenery. This small act of creating a garden had a domino effect, influencing countless individuals to embrace sustainability and adopt eco-friendly practices.

Inspiring Others

NanoMoves have a unique quality—they inspire. When someone witnesses a small, positive change, it sparks something within them. They begin to believe that they too can make a difference. Just as Sarah's community garden inspired others to plant their own, each nano-change carries the potential to ignite a spark of motivation in someone else.

Sarah's story demonstrates how her small step led to a movement. People who were initially indifferent or unaware of environmental concerns were now active participants, collectively steering the community towards a greener, more sustainable lifestyle.

THE BUTTERFLY EFFECT: A NANO-CHANGE JOURNEY

The ripple effect of a nano-change can be likened to the Butterfly Effect—a scientific theory suggesting that a small change can lead to significant alterations in a complex system. In our lives and the world around us, these small actions can amplify and resonate, creating transformative shifts. These are two transformative shifts of information.

1. Beyond our immediate reach

NanoMoves, like the flutter of a butterfly's wings, have the potential to affect outcomes beyond what we initially perceive. When you take a reusable bag to the store or opt for a vegetarian meal, you're setting a tiny precedent.

This seemingly minor action can cascade into a series of eco-conscious choices, influencing supply chains, reducing waste, and minimizing your carbon footprint. Imagine the impact when millions of individuals adopt similar habits. The collective influence of nano-changes can steer industries, drive policy changes, and shape a sustainable future.

2. Connecting Communities

NanoMoves have the remarkable ability to connect communities and create networks of change. When individuals unite through shared beliefs and actions, the collective force becomes a catalyst for even more significant transformations. A simple act of starting a recycling initiative in a neighborhood, for instance, can inspire neighboring communities to do the same.

This interconnected web of change exemplifies how nano-changes, propagated through individuals and communities, can coalesce into a powerful force for progress and positive transformation.

EMBRACING NANO-CHANGE: A CALL TO ACTION

As we navigate our lives, we often underestimate the influence of small, deliberate actions. However, the cumulative power of nano-changes is profound. By embracing these small adjustments, we not only improve ourselves but also contribute to a global shift towards a better world.

1. **Start with One Small Change**

   Begin your journey of "NanoMoves" by identifying one aspect of your life or community that you'd like to improve. Whether it's reducing waste, increasing physical activity, or fostering stronger relationships, choose one area where you can introduce a small, positive change.

2. **Spread the Ripple Effect**

Share your nano-change and the impact it has on your life with others. Encourage them to embark on their own nano-change journeys. Through dialogue and sharing experiences, we can inspire and support one another, collectively amplifying our positive influence.

By understanding and harnessing the power of nano-changes, we unlock the potential for colossal waves of positive impact. Each nano-move we make, however small, has the potential to join a vast sea of positive transformation. Together, we can shape a world that thrives on these intentional, transformative ripples. Are you ready to unleash your own nano-waves of change? Apply these principles dear reader.

CHAPTER 7

THE NANO-CHANGE MINDSETS: UNLOCKING THE POWER OF THE LAW OF AWARENESS

In the world of "NanoMoves" there exists a fundamental principle that underpins their effectiveness, guiding us toward remarkable transformation: the Law of Awareness. Chapter 7 explores the essence of this law and the NanoChange Mindsets that accompany it. As we delve into the intricacies of this concept, we will discover how heightened awareness can catalyze profound change.

THE LAW OF AWARENESS

The Law of Awareness is a simple yet potent principle. It dictates that the extent to which you are aware of your actions, thoughts, and surroundings directly influences your capacity to enact change. It serves as the foundation upon which the NanoChange philosophy is built, emphasizing the importance of consciousness and intentionality in the pursuit of personal and professional growth.

Consider the case of Michael for example, a driven executive in a fast-paced corporate world. Michael's life was a whirlwind of meetings, deadlines, and never-ending demands. His ambition and dedication were commendable, yet he found himself yearning for a sense of balance and purpose. It was the Law of Awareness that initiated his transformation.

Michael embarked on a journey of self-discovery, starting with a simple practice of mindfulness meditation. This practice cultivated a heightened sense of awareness within him. As he became attuned to the present moment, he gained clarity about his goals, values, and the changes he wished to make. This awareness laid the foundation for his NanoChange Mindset, empowering him to take conscious actions toward achieving his aspirations.

THE NANO-CHANGE MINDSETS

The NanoChange Mindsets are a set of principles that complement the Law of Awareness. They are the lenses through which we view our actions, decisions, and progress, and they encompass the following.

1. *Mindful Presence*

"Mindful Presence" encourages us to be fully engaged in the present moment. In a world characterized by distractions, it is easy to lose touch with the here and now. By cultivating mindfulness, we gain clarity, focus, and a profound sense of awareness that enables us to make deliberate, impactful NanoMoves. Mindful Presence instills the power to appreciate the beauty in small actions and transformations.

2. *Purpose-Driven Action*

The "Purpose-Driven Action" mindset prompts us to align our NanoMoves with our long-term objectives and values. It reminds us that change for the sake of change is not transformation; it is merely fluctuation. By defining our purpose, we channel our energy into NanoMoves that are not only impactful but also resonate with our deeper intentions.

3. *Reflective Learning*

"Reflective Learning" encourages us to view every action, whether successful or not, as an opportunity to learn and grow. This mindset entails self-awareness and an openness to feedback. It shifts our perspective from fearing mistakes to embracing them as stepping stones on our journey to "Expertise Elevation." With each NanoMove, you can gain insights that help you adjust and refine your approach.

4. *Adaptive Resilience*

The "Adaptive Resilience" mindset is the embodiment of our ability to overcome obstacles and adapt to change. It reminds us that in the pursuit of expertise, you will encounter setbacks and challenges. However, these are not roadblocks but opportunities to refine your NanoMoves. With the resilience mindset, we acknowledge difficulties as necessary elements of the transformation process.

5.   *Gratitude and Abundance*

The "Gratitude and Abundance" encourage us to appreciate the resources, opportunities, and people that support our journey. This mindset serves as a reminder that our progress is not solely self-driven but enriched by the interconnectedness of our lives. When we adopt an attitude of gratitude and abundance, we become more open to embracing NanoMoves that foster collaboration, empathy, and shared growth

THE POWER OF MINDSETS IN NANO-CHANGE

The NanoChange Mindsets are more than just philosophical concepts; they are the lenses through which we view and navigate our lives. When embraced collectively, these mindsets can dramatically amplify the effectiveness of NanoMoves. Each mindset contributes to an enriched sense of awareness and intentionality in our actions.

The example I gave of Michael, the ambitious executive, illustrates the transformative potential of these mindsets. His journey toward "Expertise Elevation" was catalyzed by Mindful Presence, Purpose-Driven Action, Reflective Learning, Adaptive Resilience, and Gratitude and Abundance. As he internalized these mindsets, they became the compass that guided his NanoMoves. As you embark on your own journey of "NanoMoves" , remember the profound impact that the Law of Awareness and the NanoChange Mindsets can have on your transformation. Embrace them as integral components of your toolkit, allowing you to wield the power of conscious, deliberate, and impactful change.

CHAPTER 8

NANO-CHANGE FOR PERSONAL GROWTH AND ACCOMPLISHMENTS

In our quest for success and personal growth, we often envision monumental transformations and significant life changes. We set ambitious goals, hoping to revolutionize our lives overnight. While these grand ambitions are undoubtedly inspirational, it's the subtle and consistent "Nano-Changes" that often serve as the bedrock for profound personal growth and accomplishments. Personal growth is very essential.

THE DOMINO EFFECT

One of the remarkable features of "Nano-Change" is the domino effect it can trigger in our lives. When we make small, targeted adjustments in one area, they often spill over into other facets of our existence. Let's explore this concept through the journey of Mark for example, an individual yearning for a healthier lifestyle.

Mark had long wanted to improve his health and fitness, but he felt daunted by the prospect of overhauling his diet and exercise routines. The concept of "Nano-Change" came to his rescue. Instead of committing to an intense workout regimen or a strict diet, Mark decided to make a few minor adjustments to his daily life. replaced his afternoon soda with water and started packing healthier snacks for his breaks. Gradually, he incorporated more fresh fruits and vegetables into his meals. These "Nano-Changes" had a transformative impact on Mark's health. He found himself with more energy, better concentration at work, and improved overall well-being. As he continued to make these subtle adjustments, he discovered a growing passion for exercise. The stairs were no longer a chore but a welcomed challenge, and his preference for water over sugary drinks was now a habit. Mark's story highlights how one "Nano-Change" can set off a chain reaction of healthier choices and lead to a lifestyle marked by fitness and vitality.

What small adjustments can you make today that will lead to remarkable growth and accomplishments tomorrow? The power is in your hands, and the journey is just beginning.

CHAPTER 9

NANO-CHANGE IN RELATIONSHIP AND COMMUNICATION

In our speedy, interconnected world, the nature of our connections and correspondence assumes a vital part in our regular routines. The capacity to make even the littlest, key changes, known as "Nano-Change," can essentially influence our cooperations with others. This part digs into the domain of connections and correspondence, featuring how the idea of "Nano-Change" can upset our associations with companions, family, and partners.

Relationships are intricate tapestries woven with threads of communication, trust, and understanding. In these intricate webs, seemingly insignificant actions and adjustments can have profound effects. These are the "Nano-Changes" that, when thoughtfully applied, can strengthen bonds and resolve conflicts.

Nano-Changes in communication often revolve around active listening, empathy, and effective expression. It might be a matter of pausing to truly understand what the other person is saying or employing empathy to put yourself in their shoes. It could also be about using your words more carefully, avoiding misunderstandings, and fostering clarity. These small changes can add up to create a climate of healthy, open communication.

NAVIGATING CONFLICTS

One area where Nano-Change excels is in the realm of conflict resolution. Misunderstandings and disagreements are a natural part of human interaction. However, how we handle these conflicts can determine the course of our relationships. Instead of employing large, sweeping gestures or arguments, "Nano-Change" encourages subtler actions.

Rather than reacting impulsively to a conflict, try taking a moment to reflect and respond thoughtfully. This simple pause can defuse tension and prevent escalation.

Additionally, use your words carefully, focusing on "I" statements to express your feelings and perspective, rather than pointing fingers with "You" statements.

BUILDING TRUST AND CONNECTION

Trust is the foundation of any healthy relationship. Small gestures, like being reliable and punctual, can cultivate trust over time. By consistently delivering on your promises and showing up for others, you create an environment of reliability that fosters trust. Nano-Change is also about paying attention to non-verbal cues, like maintaining eye contact and using open body language, which can communicate trustworthiness. Furthermore, building a connection with others involves showing genuine interest in their lives and experiences. Taking time to ask about their day, showing empathy, and remembering the details that matter to them can create a deeper, more meaningful connection.

ACTIVE LISTENING

A key component of Nano-Change in communication is active listening. In our fast-paced world, people often listen to respond, rather than to understand. Active listening involves truly paying attention to the speaker, asking clarifying questions, and paraphrasing to confirm understanding. It's a small change, but it can drastically improve the quality of your conversations. Your ability to listen and understand, is your capacity to handle any form of problem. When you actively listen, you make the speaker feel valued and heard. This, in turn, can lead to more open and meaningful dialogues. By being present in the moment, you enhance your ability to connect and empathize with the person you're communicating with.

COMMUNICATING WITH EMPATHY

Empathy is another vital component of effective communication. It involves understanding and sharing the feelings of another person. A Nano-Change in communication is to consciously practice empathy. Put yourself in the other person's shoes and consider how they might feel in a given situation. Empathy helps foster understanding and emotional connection. It encourages a more supportive, compassionate atmosphere, whether you're dealing with friends, family, or colleagues. When you convey empathy, you validate the other person's feelings and experiences, which can go a long way in building strong relationships.

ADAPTING TO DIFFERENT STYLE

Every individual has a one of a kind correspondence style and inclinations. A strong Nano-Change is adjusting your correspondence style to the individual you're communicating with. Certain individuals might lean toward immediate and compact correspondence, while others value more nitty gritty clarifications. By perceiving these distinctions and changing your methodology, you can work on the adequacy of your correspondence. This versatile methodology can limit false impressions and work on your capacity to really pass on your message. It exhibits regard for the other individual's inclinations and shows that you esteem their feedback.

Closing this chapter, understand that in the domain of connections and correspondence, "Nano-Change" is an awe-inspiring phenomenon. Little, deliberate changes in correspondence and conduct can essentially upgrade the nature of our associations and resolve clashes. By embracing the force of Nano-Change, we can make a universe of better, more compassionate, and valuable correspondence with everyone around us. Whether it's in our own or proficient lives, these unpretentious movements can prompt significant enhancements, at last hoisting the nature of our connections and correspondence.

CHAPTER 10

SUSTAINABLE SUCCESS: COMMINGLING NANO-CHANGE IN YOUR LIFE

In this chapter, we delve into the concept of "Sustainable Success" by integrating these "NanoChange" into your life.

Understanding Sustainable Success

Traditional notions of success often revolve around achieving significant milestones or major accomplishments. We celebrate promotions, awards, and other major achievements, yet these moments can be fleeting. Sustainable success, on the other hand, is about cultivating a way of life that continually propels you forward, providing a steady stream of accomplishments, personal satisfaction, and ongoing growth.

The Paradox of Nano-Change

The paradox of "NanoChange" lies in its subtlety. It's not about making dramatic, life-altering decisions every day. Instead, it's the practice of consistently and consciously making small, incremental adjustments. This approach allows you to navigate your life like a skilled captain steering a ship through calm waters rather than battling raging storms.

Implementing Nano-Change for Sustainable Success

● *Daily Habits and Routines*
Begin by examining your daily habits and routines. Identify areas where small changes can lead to significant improvements. Whether it's your morning routine, exercise habits, or time management, adopting "NanoMoves" in these areas can create a ripple effect of positive change.

● *Continuous Learning*
Embrace the concept of lifelong learning. Devote time to acquiring new knowledge and skills in small, consistent doses. Read a few pages of a book each day, take short online courses, or listen to educational podcasts. Over time, these "NanoChange" will accumulate into a wealth of knowledge and expertise.

● *Relationships and Communication*
In your interactions with others, practice active listening and empathy as "NanoChange." Small gestures like maintaining eye contact, using someone's name, or offering genuine compliments can strengthen your connections and communication skills, leading to more fulfilling relationships.

- ***Health and Well-Being***

Sustainable success requires a healthy body and mind. Implement "NanoChange" by incorporating short mindfulness sessions into your day, taking regular breaks to stretch, or making healthier food choices. Over time, these small adjustments will contribute to your overall well-being.

- ***Financial Savviness***

Manage your finances with "NanoChange" in mind. Track your expenses and create a budget. Even small savings can accumulate over time, providing financial security and peace of mind.

- ***Goal Setting***

Set smaller, achievable goals as "NanoChange" along the path to your larger aspirations. Break down your objectives into manageable steps and celebrate the progress you make along the way. This not only keeps you motivated but also ensures that success is a continuous journey, not just a destination.

The Accumulation of Nano-Change

The beauty of "NanoChange" is its accumulative nature. These small adjustments may seem inconsequential in the moment, but over time, they coalesce into a powerful force that propels you toward your goals. Sustainable success is not about quick fixes or temporary achievements; it's about the ongoing journey of becoming the best version of yourself.

Overcoming Resistance

One common hurdle on the path to sustainable success is resistance to change as we have already discussed. We're often resistant to alterations, even small ones, because they take us out of our comfort zones. This resistance can manifest as procrastination, self-doubt, or even fear of the unknown. Recognizing and addressing this resistance is a crucial step in integrating "NanoChange" into your life. It's about understanding that change, no matter how small, is often met with resistance, and this resistance can be a sign that you're on the right track.

Measuring Sustainable Success

Sustainable success is not always easy to measure by traditional standards. It's not about trophies or accolades; it's about fulfillment and personal growth. Instead of focusing solely on external validation, consider measuring your success by your internal satisfaction, the quality of your relationships, and the progress you've made in the areas that matter most to you. I believe that what lies in sustaining your success is embedded in you. Your greatest success is you.

Final Thoughts

Incorporating "NanoChange" into your life for sustainable success is a journey of commitment and consistency. It's a path that defies the notion of quick fixes and celebrates the beauty of small, intentional adjustments. By applying these principles, you create a way of life where success is not a destination but an ongoing journey of becoming the best version of yourself.

CONCLUSION

My dear reader, As we draw the final brushstroke on this transformative journey, we are reminded that greatness lies not in grand gestures, but in the sum of our daily choices. In "The NanoChange Prowess," we've uncovered the profound magic concealed within the mundane, and how small, deliberate adjustments can spark extraordinary transformations. This is not a book of quick fixes or fleeting victories; it is a testament to the enduring power of incremental change. With "NanoChange Prowess" as your ally, you've learned to harness the potential within each NanoMove, turning them into catalysts of your success. The ordinary is no longer mundane; it is your canvas for impactful artistry. You've embraced "Expertise Elevation," commingling "NanoChange" seamlessly into your life, forging a path towards sustainable success. As you journey forward, remember that your canvas is ever-expanding, and your potential is limitless. In every facet of your existence, from relationships to personal growth, from health to finance, "NanoChange Prowess" remains your trusted companion. It's the art of making each moment count, of weaving the ordinary into a tapestry of extraordinary achievements. In the grand tapestry of life, "The NanoChange Prowess" has been your palette, and you, the master artist. Now, as you step beyond these pages, continue to paint your masterpiece one "NanoChange" at

a time, knowing that the ordinary is but a canvas for your Maximum Impact. The world awaits the transformative strokes
of your potential, talents, and intelligence.

Quote to remember: " Your Greatest Success is YOU "

www.ingramcontent.com/pod-product-compliance
Lightning Source LLC
Chambersburg PA
CBHW061000260726
48661CB00005B/1975